D1495327

Other Giftbooks by Exley

Love Quotations
To my very Special Love
True Love …
To my very special Wife

Love a Celebration
A Token of Love
Our Love Story
To my very special Husband

Published simultaneously in 1995 by Exley Publications in Great Britain, and Exley Giftbooks in the USA.

12 11 10 9 8 7 6 5 4 3 2

Copyright © Helen Exley 1995

ISBN 1-85015-645-X

Edited and pictures selected by Helen Exley.
Designed by Pinpoint Design.
Picture research by P. A. Goldberg and J. M. Clift, Image Select, London.
Typeset by Delta, Watford.
Printed and bound in Spain by Grafo S.A., Bilbao.

Exley Publications Ltd, 16 Chalk Hill, Watford, Herts WD1 4BN, United Kingdom.

Exley Giftbooks, 232 Madison Avenue, Suite 1206, New York, NY 10016, USA.

Acknowledgements: The publishers are grateful for permission to reproduce copyright material. While every effort has been made to trace copyright holders, the publishers would be pleased to hear from any not here acknowledged. WILLIAM CANE: extract from "The Books Of Kisses" published by St. Martin's Press, New York © 1993 William Cane; ROSEMARIE JARSKI: extract from "A Kiss" published by Ebury Press Ltd. a division of Random House (UK) Ltd. © 1994 Rosemarie Jarski 1994; D. H. LAWRENCE: extracts from "Mr Noon" and "The Rainbow" reprinted by Laurence Pollinger Ltd. on behalf of The Estate of Frieda Lawrence Ravagli; JACQUES PREVERT: "The Garden" from "Paroles" © 1972 Editions Gallimard.
Picture credits: Exley Publications is very grateful to the following individuals and organizations for permission to reproduce their pictures: Archiv für Kunst (AKG), Art Resource (AR), Bridgeman Art Library (BAL), Christies Images (CI), Fine Art Photographic Library (FAP). Cover: J. W. Waterhouse, *The awakening of Adonis*, CI; title page: BAL; page 7: BAL; page 9: AKG; page 11: BAL; page 12: BAL; page 14: AKG; page 16: AKG; page 19: BAL; page 20: © 1995 Bill Brauer; page 23: AKG; page 25: BAL; page 27: AKG; page 29: SCA; page 30: © 1995 Otto Muller, Max Lutze Collection, Hamburg, BAL; page 33 © 1995 Bill Brauer; page 34: BAL; page 37: AKG; page 38: AKG; page 40: AR; page 43: AKG; page 44: AKG; page 47: FAP; page 49: AR; page 51: © 1995 Maurice Greiffenhagen, Walker Art Gallery, Liverpool, BAL; page 52: © 1995 Bill Brauer; page 55: FAP; page 56: AKG; page 59: AKG; page 60: BAL.

THE *Kiss*

Lovers'
Quotations
and
Romantic
Paintings

Edited by
HELEN EXLEY

EXLEY
NEW YORK · WATFORD UK

7he kiss is as old as the creation, and yet as young and fresh as ever. It pre-existed, still exists, and always will exist. Depend upon it, Eve learned it in Paradise, and was taught its beauties, virtues, and varieties by an angel, there is something so transcendent in it.

HALIBURTON (1796-1865)

Some say kissing is a sin; but if it was not lawful, lawyers would not allow it; if it were not holy, ministers would not do it; if it was not modest, maidens would not take it; if it was not plenty, poor folk would not get it.

ROBERT BURNS (1756-1796)

You must remember this, a kiss is still a kiss,
A sigh is just a sigh;
The fundamental things apply
As time goes by.

HERMAN HUPFELD, FROM *"EVERYBODY'S WELCOME"*
ALSO IN THE MOVIE *"CASABLANCA"*

When a clumsy cloud from here meets a fluffy little cloud from there, he billows towards her. She scurries away, and he scuds right up to her. She cries a little, and there you have your shower.
He comforts her. They spark. That's the lightning. They kiss. Thunder!

FRED ASTAIRE (1899-1987) TO GINGER ROGERS,
IN "TOP HAT"

"Now, I suppose it is proper to return each other's letters," said he. "Correct," she answered, "but let me ask if it would not be just as proper to give back all the kisses we have exchanged?"
And so they did, whereupon they immediately renewed the engagement.

TWO DANISH LOVERS

She (as he steals a kiss): "Why, you robber! I shall have you arrested for larceny from the person."
He (kissing her once more): "Very well, I have given it back. If you make that complaint against me, I shall charge you with receiving stolen property, knowing it to be such."

FROM "FUNNY JOKES"

The sound of a kiss is not so loud as that of a cannon, but its echo lasts a great deal longer.

DR. OLIVER WENDELL HOLMES (1809-1894),
FROM *"THE PROFESSOR AT THE BREAKFAST TABLE"*

It is pretty well established that lovers handle the supply of kisses very lavishly. They give them and take them with infinite disregard of possible consequences. And still – and herein we see the wonderful quality of the kiss – they retain the same intoxicating freshness as at the beginning. In love everything is mutual, but every demonstration of the passion contains something new and rejuvenating, no matter how many times the same demonstration has taken place before.

PROFESSOR CHRISTOPHER NYROP

$\mathcal{I}$t is the passion that is in the kiss that gives to it its sweetness; it is the affection in a kiss that sanctifies it.

CHRISTIAN
NESTELL
BOVEE

When they kissed it
seemed as if they did
indeed imbibe each other,
as if each were wine to the
other's thirst.

ROBERT SPEAIGHT,
FROM "THE
UNBROKEN HEART"

What is a kisse? Why this, as some approve;
The sure sweet cement, glue and lime of love.

ROBERT HERRICK (1591-1674),
FROM "A KISS"

he dictionary says that a kiss is "a salute made by touching with the lips pressed closely together and suddenly parting them." From this it is quite obvious that, although a dictionary may know something about words, it knows nothing about kissing.

HUGH MORRIS, FROM *"THE ART OF KISSING"*

What is a kiss?... The lips must pout slightly, and touch the cheek softly, and then they just part, and the job is complete. There is a kiss in the abstract! View it in the abstract. Take it as it stands!

Look at it philosophically. What is there in it? Millions upon millions have been plunged into misery and despair by this kissing; and yet when you look at the character of the thing, it is simply pouting and parting of the lips.

ANONYMOUS, 1904

A kiss is produced by a kind of sucking movement of the muscles of the lips, accompanied by a weaker or louder sound. It must be in contact with a creature or object, otherwise you could be calling a horse.

PROFESSOR CHRISTOPHER NYROP

*T*HE DECISION TO KISS FOR THE FIRST TIME
IS THE MOST CRUCIAL IN ANY LOVE STORY. IT
CHANGES THE RELATIONSHIP OF TWO PEOPLE
MUCH MORE STRONGLY THAN EVEN THE FINAL
SURRENDER, BECAUSE THIS KISS ALREADY HAS
WITHIN IT THAT SURRENDER.

EMIL LUDWIG (1861-1948), FROM *"OF LIFE AND LOVE"*

SO SWEET LOVE SEEMED THAT APRIL MORN,
WHEN FIRST WE KISSED BESIDE THE THORN,
SO STRANGELY SWEET, IT WAS NOT STRANGE
WE THOUGHT THAT LOVE COULD NEVER
CHANGE.

ROBERT BRIDGES (1844-1930)

IN A KISS, TWO SPIRITS MEET, MINGLE AND
BECOME ONE; AND AS A RESULT THERE ARISES IN
THE MIND A WONDERFUL FEELING OF DELIGHT
THAT AWAKENS AND BINDS TOGETHER THE LOVE
OF THEM THAT KISS.

AELRED OF RIEVAULX,
FROM *"TREATISE ON SPIRITUAL FRIENDSHIP"*

*I*t is a strange and a beautiful thing – first innocent love.... – all may be gazed upon with impunity ninety-nine times, and the hundredth you are a gone man. On a sudden the eye strikes you as deeper and brighter than ever; or you fancy that a long look is stolen at you beneath a drooping eyelid, and that there is a slight flush on the cheek, – and at once you are in love.

Then you spend the mornings in contriving apologies for calling, and the days and evenings in playing them off. This goes on for months, varied by the occasional daring of kissing a flower with which she presents you – perhaps in the daring intoxication of love wafting it towards her; or in an affectation of the Quixote style, kneeling with mock heroic emphasis to kiss her

hand in affected jest; and the next time you meet with her, both are stately and reserved as ever. 'Till at last on some unnoticeable day, when you find yourself alone with the lady, you quite unawares feel her hand in yours, a yielding shudder crosses her, you know not how, she is in your arms and you press upon her lips delayed but not withheld.

A long, long, kiss of youth and love.

TAIT'S EDINBURGH MAGAZINE, 1832

I clasp thy waist; I feel thy bosom's beat.
O, kiss me into faintness, sweet and dim.

ALEXANDER
SMITH
(1830-1867)

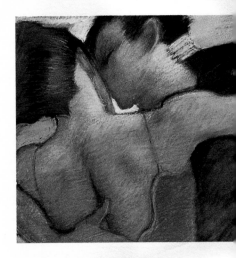

Our spirits rushed together at the touching of the lips.

ALFRED, LORD
TENNYSON
(1809-1892)

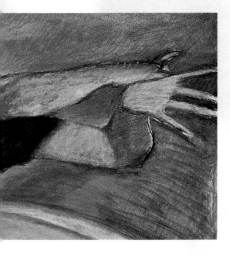

They look at each other with their mouths.
They look at each other with their whole bodies.

MURIEL RUKEYSER
(1913-1980)

*A*ll the time I have been thinking of an armchair made for two, in front of a huge crackling fire, the wireless playing some tuneful tunes, and the firelight making shadows on the walls.

Fire watching night!

a hectic ruff and tumble and then sweet reconciliation.

a terribly beautiful hug and then clasped in your arms, my head on your breast, something I am longing for now, a kiss that makes time stand still.

PAMELA MOORE

*M*an is the slave of the kiss. With a kiss a woman can tame the wildest man. By a kiss the strongest man's will becomes soft as wax.

JOACHINDA BELLAY

You are the most beautiful girl that has ever lived, and it is worth dying to have kissed you.

DYLAN THOMAS (1914-1953)

A man had given all other bliss,
And all his worldly worth for this,
To waste his whole heart in one
   kiss
Upon her perfect lips.

ALFRED, LORD TENNYSON (1809-1892),
FROM *"SIR LAUNCELOT AND
QUEEN GUINEVERE"*

There is a kiss of welcome and of parting; the long, lingering, loving, present one; the stolen or mutual one; the kiss of love, of joy, and of sorrow; the seal of promise and receipt of fulfillment. Is it strange, therefore, that a woman is invincible whose armory consists of kisses, smiles, sighs and tears?

HALIBURTON (1796-1865)

THESE KISSES ARE WHAT YOU LIVE FOR. THEY MAKE YOU LITERALLY ACHE WITH PLEASURE. THEY LIGHT YOU UP AND SEND SHOCKS THROUGH YOUR NERVES FOR HOURS AND DAYS AFTERWARD. THEY HAVE YOU LAUGHING AND CRYING AND DOUBTING YOUR SANITY AND WANTING TO STAY UP ALL NIGHT JUST SO YOU CAN REMEMBER THEM. THE MAGIC THAT TRANSFORMS THESE KISSES IS THE STUFF OF ROMANCE. THEY ARE MUCH MORE LIKELY TO OCCUR IN A ROMANTIC SETTING, UNDER MOONLIGHT, ON A BEACH, AT FIRESIDE, OR IN A SPOT THAT HAS SPECIAL MEANING FOR BOTH LOVERS....

WILLIAM CANE, FROM *"THE BOOK OF KISSES"*

*E*leanor!" he again exclaimed; and in a moment he had her clasped to his bosom. How this was done, whether the doing was with him or her, whether she had flown thither conquered by the tenderness of his voice, or he with a violence not likely to give offence had drawn her to his breast, neither knew; nor can I declare. There was now a sympathy between them which hardly admitted of individual motion. They were one and the same, – one flesh, – one spirit, – one life.

ANTHONY TROLLOPE (1815-1882)

And our lips found ways

of speaking

What words cannot say,

Till a hundred nests gave music,

And the East was gray.

FREDERICK LAWRENCE KNOWLES
(1869-1905), FROM *"A MEMORY"*

... he kissed her softly, her hair,
her face, her ears, gently, softly,
like dew falling.

D. H. LAWRENCE (1885-1930)

*Only he felt he could no more
dissemble,
And kissed her, mouth to mouth,
all in a tremble.*

LEIGH HUNT (1784-1859),
FROM *"STORY OF RIMINI"*

*A kiss is strange. It's a living
thing, a communication, a whole
wild emotion expressed in a simple
moist touch.*

MICKEY SPILLANE, b.1918,
FROM *"THE KILLING MAN"*

*Kiss me as if you made believe
You were not sure, this eve,
How my face, your flower,
had pursed
Its petals up; so, here and there
You brush it, till I grow aware
Who wants me, and wide open
I burst.*

ROBERT BROWNING (1812-1889),
FROM *"IN A GONDOLA"*

he kiss is a wordless articulation of desire whose object lies in the future, and somewhat to the south.

LANCE MORROW

The one who grants a kiss grants something else, and any one who has free access to kisses has access to more.

PETER SYV

I said, "He's too old, he has too many children and I'm not interested."... [Then] he kissed me on the back of my neck, and it sent this rush through me, and I went, "Oh, shoot."

MISSY THORNEBURG,
WIFE OF MILLIONAIRE "BIG JIM" THORNEBURG

"May I print a kiss on your lips?" I said,
* And she nodded her full permission;*
So we went to press and I rather guess
* We printed a full edition.*

JOSEPH LILIENTHAL, FROM *"A FULL EDITION"*

*L*ove's favorite pastime is the progressive kiss.

When a man woos a woman he usually begins demonstrations by kissing her gloved hands – an innocent enough act surely.

But it does not long satisfy him. The glove is in the way, and he longs to press his lips to her soft flesh – the white fingers first – then the pink palm, and the blue veined wrist.

She blushes a little at this and draws her hand away, yet, surely, it is not very wrong, she thinks.

After that he begs to kiss her cheek – just one little touch of the lips to its velvet surface – no more. Such a tiny favor to ask? And if one cheek is caressed, why not the other? It is unfair to show favoritism. Crossing from the left cheek to the right, leads directly over love's domain – the lips, the home of kisses.

ELLA WHEELER WILCOX
(1850-1919)

THE GARDEN

Thousands and thousands of years

Would never suffice

To entice

That small second of eternity

When you kissed me

When I kissed you

One morning in the light of winter

In Parc Montsouris in Paris

In Paris

On Earth

Earth that is a star.

JACQUES PRÉVERT (1900-1977)

*H*e glared at her a moment
through the dusk, and the next
instant she felt his arms about
her and his lips on her own lips.
His kiss was like white lightning,
a flash that spread, and spread
again, and stayed.

HENRY JAMES (1843-1916),
FROM *"THE PORTRAIT OF A LADY"*

On taking the necessary step from the sublime, we have the description by a lady of her feelings on being kissed for the first time. She felt like a tub of butter swimming in honey, cologne, nutmegs, and cranberries, and as though something was running through her nerves on feet of diamonds, escorted by several little cupids in chariots drawn by angels, shaded with honeysuckles and the whole spread with melted rainbows!

J. BRANDER MATTHEWS

... Down there we sat upon the Moss.
And did begin to play
A Thousand Amorous Tricks, to pass
The heat of the day.
A many Kisses he did give:
and I return'd the same
Which made me willing to receive
  That which I dare not name.

APHRA BEHN (1640-1689), FROM *"THE WILLING MISTRISS"*

"I am in favour of preserving the French habit of
kissing ladies' hands – after all, one must start
somewhere."

SACHA GUITRY (1885-1957)

She that will kiss, they say, will do worse.

ROBERT DAVENPORT (1623-1639), FROM *"CITY NIGHT CAP"*

Kisses are like grains of gold or silver found upon
the ground, of no value themselves, but precious as
showing that a mine is near.

GEORGE VILLIERS (1628-1687)

She embraces me elaborately,... casually as a breeze, softly as one caresses a flower; she kisses me as dispassionately as heaven kisses the sea, softly and quietly as dew kisses a flower, solemnly as the sea kisses the image of the moon.

SÖREN KIERKEGAARD (1813-1855)

I kiss you firmly a hundred times, embrace you tenderly and am sketching in my imagination various pictures in which you and I figure, and nobody and nothing else.

ANTON CHEKHOV (1816-1904),
TO OLGA CHEKHOV

*H*is mouth wandered, wandered,
almost touched her ear, She felt the
first deep flame run over her.... He
had found the soft down that lay back
beyond her cheeks, near the roots of
her ears. And his mouth stirred it
delicately, as infernal angels stir the
fires with glass rods, or a dog on the
scent stirs the grass till the game
starts from cover.

D. H. LAWRENCE (1885-1930), FROM *"MR. NOON"*

I looked in her eyes and put my arm
around her as I had before and kissed
her. I kissed her hard and held her
tight and tried to open her lips; they
were closed tight... I held her close
against me and could feel her heart
beating and her lips opened and her
head went back against my hand and
then she was crying on my shoulder.

ERNEST HEMINGWAY (1898-1961),
FROM *"FAREWELL TO ARMS"*

*S*o long as there is true, pure love in the world, kissing will continue to be one of the very finest pastimes of lovers.... Its music is the melody of the heart and the poetry of the soul. Its rapture is the charm of youth, the joy of manhood and the beatitude of old age.

ALFRED FOWLER, FROM *"THE CURIOSITIES OF KISSING"*

Birds do it. Bugs do it. Even snooker-balls and slugs do it. But only you and I do it for love. From its origins in "kiss-feeding", kissing has evolved beyond the nutritional imperative, through primitive tribal rituals, by way of troubadours, courtly love and Hollywood, surviving *en route* religious bans, anti-kissing leagues and garlic-dip to become what it is today, the most perfect expression of love between two human beings.

ROSEMARIE JARSKI

O LOVE! O FIRE! ONCE HE DREW
WITH ONE LONG KISS MY WHOLE SOUL THROUGH
MY LIPS, AS SUNLIGHT DRINKETH DEW.

ALFRED, LORD TENNYSON (1809-1892)

HE KNEW THAT WHEN HE KISSED THIS GIRL, HIS
MIND WOULD NEVER ROMP AGAIN LIKE THE
MIND OF GOD....
THEN HE KISSED HER. AT HIS LIPS' TOUCH SHE
BLOSSOMED FOR HIM LIKE A FLOWER AND THE
INCARNATION WAS COMPLETE.

F. SCOTT-FITZGERALD (1896-1940),
FROM *"THE GREAT GATSBY"*

AND WHEN MY LIPS MEET THINE,
THY VERY SOUL IS WEDDED UNTO MINE.

H. H. BOYESEN (1848-1895), FROM *"THY GRACIOUS FACE"*

THEIR LIPS DREW NEAR, AND CLUNG INTO A KISS;
A LONG, LONG KISS, A KISS OF YOUTH AND LOVE ...
EACH KISS A HEART-QUAKE....

LORD BYRON (1788-1824), FROM *"DON JUAN"*

A Kiss In The Rain

One stormy morn I chanced to meet
   A lassie in the town;
Her locks were like the ripened wheat,
   Her laughing eyes were brown.
I watched her as she tripped along
   Till madness filled my brain,
And then – and then – I know 'twas wrong –
   I kissed her in the rain!

Oh, let the clouds grow dark above,
   My heart is light below;
'Tis always summer when we love,
   However winds may blow;
And I'm as proud as any prince,
   All honors I disdain:
She says I am her *rain beau* since
   I kissed her in the rain.

SAMUEL MINTURN PECK (1854-1938)

*B*UT HIS MOUTH WAS ALREADY SLANTING

ACROSS HERS, AND HE'D ALREADY ENSURED

THERE'D BE NO ESCAPE FROM IT. LEISURELY,

WITH INFINITE CARE, HE BESTOWED ON HER THE

FINESSE OF A LIFETIME, KISSES MEANT TO

ENTICE, TO MESMERIZE, TO TAP EVERY SENSUAL

IMPULSE SHE POSSESSED. HER ARMS WERE

ALREADY ENCIRCLING HIS NECK WHEN HIS

TONGUE SEDUCED HER LIPS TO PART, ENTERED,

AND TOOK HER SWIFTLY TO THAT REALM OF NOT-

CARING-WHAT-HE DID.

JOHANNA LINDSEY, FROM *"GENTLE ROGUE"*

*Y*ou want to know how many kisses would be enough for me, Lesbia? The number of sand grains between the tombs of Libya's ancient lords and the temples where Egypt worships Jove in the shape of a ram. The number of stars that watch the furtive love affairs of humankind while the night is passing over them in silence. That's how many would satisfy your crazed Catullus. What can't be counted can't be an unlucky number.

CATULLUS, (C.84-54 B.C.), *"POEM VII"*

"Do not ask, Lesbia," sings Catullus, "how many kissings of thine can be enough? ... as many as are the sands of the African desert; or as many as are the stars that behold the secret loves of mortals when night is still."

CATULLUS (C. 84-54 B.C.)

Give me a kisse and to that kisse a score;
Then to that twenty, add a hundred more:
And thousand to that hundred: so kisse on,
    To make that thousand up a million;
Treble that million, and when that is done,
Let's kisse afresh, as when we first begun."

ROBERT HERRICK (1591-1674),
FROM *"TO ANTHEA: OH, MY ANTHEA"*

... they stood still under the trees, whilst his lips waited on her face, waited like a butterfly that does not move on a flower. She pressed her breast a little nearer to him, he moved, put both his arms round her and drew her close.

And then, in the darkness, he bent to her mouth, softly, and touched her mouth with his mouth. She was afraid, she lay still on his arm, feeling his lips on her lips. She kept still, helpless. Then his mouth drew near, pressing open her mouth, a hot drenching surge rose within her, she opened her lips to him, in pained poignant eddies she drew him nearer, she let him come further, his lips came and surging, surging, soft, oh soft, yet oh, like the powerful surge of water, irresistible, till with a little blind cry, she broke away.

D. H. LAWRENCE (1885-1930), FROM *"THE RAINBOW"*

When soul meets soul on lovers' lips.

PERCY BYSSHE SHELLEY (1792-1822),
FROM *"PROMETHEUS UNBOUND"*

They saw each other's dark eyes darting light
Into each other – and, beholding this,
Their lips drew near and clung into a kiss.

They had not spoken, but they felt allured,
As if their lips and souls each other beckon'd,
Which, being joined, like swarming bees they clung
Their hearts the flowers from whence the honey
sprung.

LORD BYRON (1788-1824), FROM *"DON JUAN"*

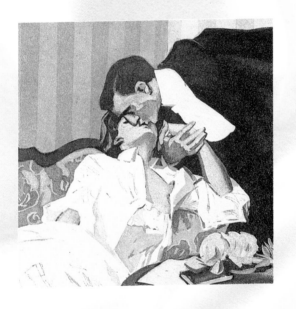

We have the memory of one we received in our youth, which lasted us forty years and we believe it will be one of the last things we shall think of when we die.

REV. SIDNEY SMITH

When age chills the blood, when our pleasures are past –

For years fleet away with the wings of the dove –

The dearest remembrance will still be the last,

Our sweetest memorial the first kiss of love.

LORD BYRON (1788-1824), FROM *"THE FIRST KISS OF LOVE"*